I0101594

*To*

_____

*From*

_____

*Date*

_____

# THE PURSUIT OF PURPOSE

## Maximizing God's Blueprint For Fulfilling Your Destiny

## Michael Lipede

**THE CORNERSTONE PUBLISHING**

**THE PURSUIT OF PURPOSE**
Copyright © 2020 by **Michael  Lipede**

ISBN: 978-1-952098-10-9

**Christian Growth Series**
is an arm of the Teaching Ministry of Michael O
Lipede
4858 Steamboat Lake Court,
Colorado Springs, CO 80924

**Cover Design & Book layout by:**
Cornerstone Creativity Group LLC
Phone: +1(516)-547-4999
www.thecornerstonepublishers.com

Printed in The United States of America

# *Contents*

Introduction....................................................7

1. Saved To Serve........................................11

2. Power Of Purpose..................................19

3. Discovering Your Purpose....................31

4. Habits That Nurture Destiny...............47

5. Fight For Your Purpose.........................65

The Greatest Decision................................79

# *Introduction*

Life is short. It is amazing how a decade flies by, as though it were a tick of a second. The brevity of life should urge us to make the best use of every moment. We do not have as much time on our hands as we often think we do.

A while ago, I was thinking about my growing up experiences and my childhood friends. As I did, the memory was as vivid as if the events occurred the day before. But, as I counted the years, I discovered that over 50 momentous years of my life had already been used up. It suddenly dawned on me that I didn't have as much time left for my life's assignment as I thought I had.

I believe I am not alone in this supposition. You might be equally taken aback by how much time you have spent on earth and how apparently little you have been able to achieve within that long stretch of years. Your evaluation is quite needful so that whatever time you have left can be utilized optimally.

The purposes of this book are to help every reader make the most judicious use of their time, sync with God's divine program for their lives, and attain fulfillment in the span and corner given to them by God called LIFE.

More importantly, as believers, we need to live daily with a consciousness of eternity. We will be judged on the basis of what we did with our time on earth. We will be accountable for how every second was expended in our earthly journey. With all of these at stake should we not learn how to make the best use of our time on earth?

I think we should, and this book will help accomplish that goal.

# CHAPTER 1

# SAVED TO SERVE

# Saved To Serve

*"But rise, and stand upon thy feet: for I have appeared unto thee for this* **purpose***, to make thee a minister and a witness both of these things which thou hast seen, and of those things in the which I will appear unto thee."*

**—Acts 26:16**

The year 1985 is very significant to me. In that year, Jesus salvaged me from academic wreck. In the previous year, my GPA had plummeted so badly that I had thought my entire educational ambition was doomed. I had initially nursed the dream of proceeding to the graduate school for a master's degree on graduation from college. Then, in 1984, an academic mishap occurred, which suddenly put my dream in serious jeopardy.

I had written the examination for my penultimate year after preparing very poorly. Worse still, I had suffered severe brain blockage due to excessive consumption of caffeine. I guess that was my personal reaction to caffeine. Needless to say, I performed so badly in the examination. Consequently, I became agitated by the possibility of having to drop out of college. When the results were released, somehow, I barely made it through to the final year in college, even though with the lowest GPA imaginable.

With all hope of realizing my lofty dream

of proceeding to a graduate school after graduation seemingly lost, I turned to God in earnest prayer, asking Him to turn things around in my favor. I knew that I needed a miracle if all I had hoped for would ever come true. The future was as bleak as the darkest night; I could not see any way forward. In my despondency, I held on to God, seeking His intervention.

In 1985, when I wrote my final examination, the miraculous happened. Jesus intervened, and I had the best result of my life until now. What a boost! What a resuscitation! Jesus restored my dream and revamped my hope!

## You're next in Line!

Are you going through some impossible situation? I will encourage you to turn it over to God; for, with Him, nothing is impossible (Matthew 19:26). Life will come with waves of afflictions, stiff oppositions and challenges that defy all human remedies. When all of these happen, never stand perplexed in hopeless surrender to these opposing forces. Instead, turn them over to Jesus, the one who specializes in doing the impossible.

In the midst of the storm, I had given my life to Jesus; I got born again. With the mountain of academic impossibility moved out of my way, my faith in Him was strengthened. I decided to fully commit my life to Him, in appreciation of His goodness to me. He told me that I could never claim to be committed to Him without actively serving Him. He led me to a local Assemblies of God Church in my neighborhood where I was planted for spiritual growth and service.

Itching to serve, I approached one of the leaders of the church and asked Him how I could be of service to the church. His response threw me off balance. He said I was to seek the face of the Lord in prayer until He revealed to me what He had called me to do.

That advice stirred a challenge in me. It reinforced my belief that the littlest in Christ's Kingdom could hear directly from

Him. I went into a season of periodic prayer and fasting, asking Him to tell me what my ministry was. After a while, He spoke. He told me what He called me to do and I have since stuck to His plan for my life. I have since realized that this is the Bible pattern for career, life and ministry. In Acts of Apostles 26:16 Jesus appeared to Paul for the purpose of revealing to Him what He had called him to do. This testimony lays the proper foundation for the next chapter of this book.

# CHAPTER 2

# POWER OF PURPOSE

# *Power Of Purpose*

*"The L*ORD *of hosts hath sworn, saying, Surely as I have thought, so shall it come to pass; and as I have* **purpose***d, so shall it stand"*

**—Isaiah 14:24**

Creation is a masterpiece of purposeful design. Nothing in creation is an accidental occurrence. There is no chance in creation; everything is specifically customized to suit a particular purpose.

Creation is like one big orchestra in which different musicians play different tunes but with the singular purpose of producing a delightsome musical harmony. When each player plays their tunes independently, it is noise; but when all tunes are played in harmony, it is music.

We cannot afford to be the discordant sound in the rhythm of life. We must understand how God designed life to function, assume the role the Great Composer has assigned to us and play that role as best as we can. Our divinely assigned role is our destiny or purpose.

## Locate Your Purpose.

To succeed in life and to maximally utilize the limited time we have on earth, you must find out God's purpose for your life.

Many are roaming the wilderness of life, experimenting with everything they stumble on. You need not waste your precious time on such a vain enterprise. God has a purpose for your life which has already been predetermined before you were born. The discovery of that purpose is the beginning of real living.

Quit existing and start living the true life of purpose which God has ordained for you. Doing so comes with enormous benefits and possibilities. The Scripture confirms this, as highlighted below:

## Purpose will strengthen and fortify you.

When you discover your purpose, you will never be frustrated out of the race of life. "For the LORD of hosts hath **purpose**d, and who shall disannul it? and his hand is stretched out, and who shall turn it back?" (Isaiah 14:27). It is true that you will encounter strong forces of opposition in life but, as long as you are in God's purpose, no opposition can be strong enough to reverse His plans and desires for your life.

## Purpose attracts divine backing to your life.

God always stands behind His purpose to accomplish it. You can be sure that God will ever stand so stoutly behind His purpose for your life. You know why? His integrity demands that He stands behind what He has stated or started. Whatever God says, He is bound to bring to manifestation. Whatever He originates, He will facilitate and complete.

So, if you are in God's purpose for your life, you automatically have His backing and support to see you through. God gives this assurance in Isaiah 46:10-11: "Declaring the end from the beginning, and from ancient times the things that are not yet done, saying, My counsel shall stand, and I will do all my pleasure: Calling a ravenous bird from the east, the man that executeth my counsel from a far country: yea, I have spoken it, I will also bring it to pass; I have purposed it, I will also do it."

## Purpose positions you for favor and breakthroughs.

All things, whether good or bad, will ultimately work together for your good when you are in God's purpose. "And we know that all things work together for good to them that love God, to them who are the called according to his purpose." (Romans 8:28). God, in His wisdom, will turn every mistake, weakness and opposition around in your favor if you are in the center of His will for your life.

## Purpose stimulates your passion.

Your God-given purpose will release your passion. Jesus is the perfect example of this truth. He had a burning passion to do the will of the Father because He was executing God's purpose for His life: John 2:15-17 narrates, "And when he had made a scourge of small cords, he drove them all out of the temple, and the sheep, and the oxen; and poured out the changers' money, and overthrew the tables; And said unto them that sold doves, Take these things hence; make not my Father's house an house of merchandise. And his disciples remembered that it was written, **The zeal of thine house hath eaten me up.**"

## Purpose guarantees fulfillment.

Only your purpose will give you fulfillment in life. Again, Jesus perfectly exemplified this, as recorded in John 4:31-34: "In the mean while his disciples prayed him, saying, Master, eat. But he said unto them, I have meat to eat that ye know not of. Therefore said the disciples one to another, Hath any man brought him ought to eat? Jesus saith unto them, **My meat is to do the will of him that sent me, and to finish his work.**"

To Jesus, His purpose was his food. He derived pleasure and satisfaction from pursuing His purpose. It is unfortunate that many people who are not finding fulfillment in their jobs, remain stuck to such jobs, just to earn some income. The truth, however, is that God did not design us to be enslaved to our occupations. He has, in fact, built into us innate pleasure and satisfaction that are activated the moment we begin to pursue His purpose for our lives.

## Purpose facilitates success.

Your success is in your purpose. Peter was a skilled and diligent fisherman. The only trade he knew prior to meeting Jesus was fishing. Unfortunately, that was not God's ultimate purpose for his life. It is not surprising, therefore, that, despite his assiduous labor as an astute fisherman, he was poor and unsuccessful.

In Luke 5:1-11, we see the picture of Peter as a frustrated and tired man at the brink of giving up on his trade. However, Jesus quickly came to the rescue. He redirected the ship of his life by showing him God's true purpose for his life. He had been designed from eternity to be a fisher of men, a winner of souls and a trailblazing apostle of the gospel. When he got his bearings right, the failed fisherman became one of the most successful soul-winners of all time. Your success is in your purpose.

You are probably failing at what you are doing today because you were never cut out for it.

## Purpose engenders focus.

Focus is powerful. When light rays are converged and focused at a single spot, the convergence produces a sharp cutting effect. In the same vein, when our energies are focused on a single assignment, we are more productive and effective than ever. The diffusion of our efforts on too many unrelated things at a time drains us of valuable resources. Once we discover our purpose, we must, as much as we can, avoid every distraction that calls our attention away from our purpose.

Indeed, the main benefit of purposeful living is that it helps us identify what deserves our attention and what needs to be pushed to the back burner of life. Focus will produce specialization because all your faculties will be directed to a single purpose and that concentration will produce the best of you.

## Purpose comes with divine anointing.

God anoints people to accomplish His purpose. Luke 4:18 contains a classic example of why God anoints people. In that verse, Jesus states clearly the purpose He was anointed by the Spirit of the Lord: "The Spirit of the Lord is upon me, because he hath anointed me to preach the gospel to the poor; he hath sent me to heal the brokenhearted, to preach deliverance to the captives, and recovering of sight to the blind, to set at liberty them that are bruised."

The anointing of the Holy Spirit is poured on us to accomplish our God-given purpose. God will not anoint us to do something different from His will for us. Many people have good intentions and healthy desires for being anointed but God will not anoint them until they have discovered His purpose for their lives. We need not be in ministry to be anointed, we only need to be in His purpose.

## Uniquely Crafted.

We can go on and on enumerating the benefits of identifying God's purpose for our lives. However, one point needs to be mentioned in addition to all stated above: you were designed to be you and your unique design is to accomplish a task, which only you can accomplish.

God made this clear to Jeremiah. Jeremiah did not know that his personality was predetermined to suit his calling. He tried to be evasive but God was emphatic. He told Jeremiah:

> *"Before I formed thee in the belly I knew thee; and before thou camest forth out of the womb I sanctified thee, and I ordained thee a prophet unto the nations." (Jeremiah 1:5).*

What He told Jeremiah is what he tells you now. There is nothing accidental about your creation. You are not just a random being. You are loaded with specific potentials and possibilities. You are a carrier of God's purpose to be accomplished on earth!

# CHAPTER 3

# DISCOVERING YOUR PURPOSE

CHAPTER 3

# Discovering Your Purpose

*"In whom also we have obtained an inheritance, being predestinated according to the purpose of him who worketh all things after the counsel of his own will."*

**—Ephesians 1:11**

We can never overemphasize the subject of purpose or destiny because it is the reason for our existence. It stands toweringly above all other issues of life. Discovering our purpose is like having a solid foundation upon which a house is built. A house without a good foundation will certainly crash at the slightest touch of a storm. This is the experience of many Christians who plan big in life without having the foundation of purpose in place.

I repeat, with great force, that there is a prophetic destiny or purpose hanging over your head, begging to be discovered and fulfilled. I pray that you will not leave this earth without discovering and fulfilling that purpose.

## Nature of Purpose

There is a general purpose for all Christians. I call this "our common destiny in Christ". The destiny of a cub is to become a lion. The destiny of a kitten is to become a cat. And the destiny of a poppy is to become a dog. In the same vein, the destiny of all Christians is to become like Jesus in character and mastery.

However, this is a common destiny which belongs to us collectively as a result of our spiritual genealogical connection to Christ; the Tree to which all branches attach. As important as this common destiny is, it is not the subject of our discussion. Our focus, here, is on the personal destiny of the individual Christian, which is unique to him or her.

This customized destiny or purpose, which is as peculiar to you as your finger prints are peculiar to your creation, defines your sphere of influence and dominion. It is the discovery and fulfillment of this destiny or purpose that aligns you with God's perfect will for you and guarantees your success in life. Here is an analogy to give you a clearer picture. It is generally required that all workers in a corporate environment abide by certain common prescribed codes of behavior and regulations. However, each worker has a job description, which spells out the company's expectations of the worker with regard to his or her employment. No person who veers away from their job description is considered by any means a good employee. The success of every worker depends on how well they perform in the execution of their assigned job description.

Similarly, the personal destiny of the Christian is his or her assigned job description which spells out what God created them to accomplish.

How do we discover this glorious destiny or purpose?

## Download or Receive a Vision From God

*"And Joseph dreamed a dream, and he told it his brethren: and they hated him yet the more. And he said unto them, Hear, I pray you, this dream which I have dreamed: For, behold, we were binding sheaves in the field, and, lo, my sheaf arose, and also stood upright; and, behold, your sheaves stood round about, and made obeisance to my sheaf." (Genesis 37:5-7).*

Joseph's life serves as a prototype of how God wants our lives to be lived. His successes in life can be traced to the dream he had in his teenage years. This dream was God's vision for his life. A vision is the revelation of God's plan and purpose for our lives. A dream is a vision revealed in our sleep. An open vision is a revelation usually given to us with our eyes wide open. It involves supernaturally seeing into the spirit realm with open eyes. There is also the normal vision which is given to us when our eyes are closed but we are not sleeping. The common denominator of all visions is that they are given when our senses are temporarily suspended, so that we can see into the spirit world with the eyes of our spirits.

We must note that the revelation of God's purpose for our lives need not be dramatic to be authentic. God can accomplish the same purpose which He does through a dream or an open vision, through a quiet impression of the Holy Spirit. Romans 8:14 says, "For as many as are led by the

Spirit of God, they are the sons of God."
Through an inner leading of the Holy Spirit,
God can firmly plant a vision in us. The
means through which a vision is birthed is
irrelevant; all that matters is the conviction
that we have heard from God.

## Intentionally Set Time Apart o Seek God For the Revelation of the Vision

"I will stand upon my watch, and set me
upon the tower, and will watch to see
what he will say unto me, and what I
shall answer when I am reproved. And
the LORD **answered me, and said, Write the
vision, and make it plain upon tables, that
he may run that** readeth it. For the vision is
yet for an appointed time, but at the end it
shall speak, and not lie: though it tarry, wait
for it; because it will surely come, it will not
tarry" (Habakkuk 2:1-3).

If we are truly serious about receiving God's
blueprint for our lives, we must be deliberate
in seeking His face about the matter. What
we devote our time to shows our priority.
The discovery of destiny or purpose is so

foundational to life that it should be given prime position in our list of to-do things. It is one thing that validates every other thing we do in life.

Earlier on, I gave a short testimony of my discussion with a leader in the church I joined after my initial encounter with Christ. He counseled that it was my responsibility to find out from God what His plan and purpose for my life were. After that meeting, I went into a season of intermittent fasting and prayer. The sole purpose of the exercise was to find out from God His purpose for my life. After a while, I had a dream in which the Lord Jesus appeared to me and showed me what He had called me to do.

There is nothing as assuring as hearing from the Lord directly. Every child of God has this divine access to the Heavenly Father. I frown at a practice many Christians engage in when they want to know God's will for their lives. Instead of spending quality time to seek the Lord by themselves, they would rather seek intermediaries that they consider more spiritual than they are for revelation. This practice obscures the equal access which we all have to the throne room of God by the reason of Christ's finished work. While others can confirm whatever revelation we receive from the Lord, we must realize that it is our primary duty to receive from God directly what His purpose is for our lives.

The above passage in Habakkuk is a scriptural proof of my emphasis here. The prophet Habakkuk wanted to know God's plan for the future. He decided to set time aside for his inquiry with God. He figuratively compared himself to a watchman on the watch tower who had his spiritual antennae tuned to heaven. He was so much devoted to that purpose that nothing could distract him. No wonder God responded with clarity and passion.

When we take God serious, He takes us serious. Saints, let us make seeking God ourselves a daily practice. It is the best way to cultivate a vibrant relationship with Him.

# Be Totally Devoted to the Vision Through Preparation

*"And the child grew, and waxed strong in spirit, and was in the deserts till the day of his shewing unto Israel." (Luke 1:80).*

As revealed in the book of Habakkuk, the vision is for an appointed time. God has a scheduled time for the fulfillment of whatever vision He gives to us. Jumping ahead of God, wanting to accomplish our God-given vision prematurely, has ruined many visions. The timing for the fulfillment of our God-given vision belongs to God. The scriptures were full of prophecies about the coming of the Messiah but when He came, He had to wait for 30 years before He assumed His Messianic mantle.

We must not only trust God for the revelation of the vision, we must also trust Him for the right timing. John the Baptist, forerunner of the Messiah, was born six months before Jesus. The Bible tells us that he lived in the wilderness for a long time preparing himself for the day of his showing. The day of our showing is the right time for the manifestation of our vision. Imagine a man with such a loud prophetic pronouncement about his life having to wait for 30 years before the vision given to him was fulfilled. His life teaches us some vital lessons of life. The first is that God will never entrust his work into the hands of a novice. Luke tells us that the child (John the Baptist) *grew*. Preparation days are never wasted days. From God's perspective, preparation days are more important than the days of manifestation. Secondly, preparation days are days in the desert - boring and seemingly useless but they are the days when the foundation for an enduring ministry is being laid. Lastly, the waiting period is that time when our spirit man is developed (waxed strong in spirit) and galvanized so that we will be able to carry the massive load of responsibilities that lie ahead. God will not give you a blessing that you do not have the capacity to contain. Preparation days are the days when capacities are built.

Ironically, we often grow so impatient and try to skip the process that God has put in place for our spiritual edification. We forget that the quality of our preparation determines the quality of our manifestation. Rather than being obsessed with the vision, we must invest our time in the preparation. The details of what we are expected to do during our desert or preparation days are discussed in the next chapter of this book.

## Develop a Wholesome Work Ethic

*"Servants, obey in all things your masters according to the flesh; not with eyeservice, as menpleasers; but in singleness of heart, fearing God; And whatsoever ye do, do it heartily, as to the Lord, and not unto men; Knowing that of the Lord ye shall receive the reward of the inheritance: for ye serve the Lord Christ."* (Colossians 3:22-24).

God hates tardiness. God's work is spiritual business that requires the highest level of discipline. Many people who had failed in other vocations in life because of their laziness had turned to ministry in the mistaken belief that ministry was an easy route to success. Unsurprisingly, many of such have also failed woefully in ministry because true ministry is seriously exerting. This is the reason God will test us in the natural realm before committing to us spiritual responsibilities.

Jesus, the Messiah, was a carpenter before his true call was committed to His hands. Elisha was a cattle rancher before he became a prophet. Peter was a diligent fisherman before he was called into the ministry. God will not use idle people. Everybody called to ministry in the Bible was busy doing something. He that is faithful in little is faithful in much. We cannot ascend the high pedestal of ministry when we cannot survive the challenges of mundane affairs. We cannot be lazy secular employees and think that, overnight, we will become hardworking preachers.

Our work ethic in the natural realm is a pointer to what type of ministers we will be when our vision comes into full manifestation. The truth is that, whether in secular world or ministry, we must have a wholesome work ethic; always investing our best efforts into every enterprise committed into our hands, as though God were our employer (and indeed, He is). A good work ethic is an act of worship which qualifies us for the fulfillment of our vision.

# CHAPTER 4

# HABITS THAT NURTURE DESTINY

CHAPTER 4

# Habits That Nurture Destiny

*"This book of the law shall not depart out of thy mouth; but thou shalt meditate therein day and night, that thou mayest observe to do according to all that is written therein: for then thou shalt make thy way prosperous, and then thou shalt have good success."*

**—Joshua 1:8**

Agreat vision had been committed into the hands of Joshua: "Be strong and of a good courage: for unto this people shalt thou divide for an inheritance the land, which I sware unto their fathers to give them." (Joshua 1:6). At the time he was commissioned, Joshua was the most anointed and equipped person on earth for the job. God had clearly revealed his assignment to him: he was to divide unto the children of Israel their inheritance, the Promised Land. Moses had transferred his anointing to him and the people were more than ready to support him to succeed. However, in spite of all these positive conditions surrounding him, God gave him detailed directions of what he had to do on a daily basis so that the vision and promises of God for his life could come to pass.

Many Christians receive a sure word from God about their purpose and sit down idle, expecting the vision to fulfill itself, without any corresponding action toward its fulfillment. It is not surprising that such believers wait for years and years and never witness the fulfillment of their cherished vision.

We are creatures of habits. God made us so. Unfortunately, over the years, the devil has so much corrupted the word "habit" so that, whenever it is mentioned, it rings up a negative connotation. Yet, in the true sense of it, *a habit is an acquired pattern regularly followed until it has become almost involuntary.* We get so used to doing it that it becomes a part of us.

The implication, therefore, is that not all habits are evil. There are good habits and there are bad habits. While we must do all we can to free ourselves from evil habits, we must strive to cultivate good habits that will help us get ahead in life. What you habitually do ultimately sets the pace and tone of your life. Someone once said: "Thoughts become words, words become actions, actions become habits, habits become character and character becomes destiny." Life is the sum total of what we do every day, not what we do once in a while. God wanted Joshua to cultivate success habits when He told him to meditate on His Word DAY and NIGHT. God Himself prescribed daily habits for Joshua which he must nurture if he would see the vision come to pass.

All through the Bible, we find that successful people were those who gave themselves to habits that God ordained for our success on earth. The following are 12 of these key habits that have transformed the lives of great men.

## 1. Rising Early

"And in the morning, rising up a great while before day, he went out, and departed into a solitary place, and there prayed." (Mark 1:35).

How we start the day matters. Jesus would rise very early in the morning to spend time with His Father. No wonder He experienced phenomenal successes in His life and ministry. We must be early risers, if we will succeed in life and we must spend the early hours of the day with God, if we are truly looking to Him for daily guidance and empowerment. This is an established pattern with many great men of God and visionaries, both in Bible and contemporary times.

## 2. Study Of The Word

*"Study to shew thyself approved unto God, a workman that needeth not to be ashamed, rightly dividing the word of truth." (2 Timothy 2:15).*

Ignorance is the bane of the doomed. The Bible says God's people perish for lack of knowledge. Many problems remain mysteries to us because we are not sufficiently equipped with adequate knowledge to tackle them. Merely using a can opener can be a big problem to people who have not seen one before. We cannot ascend beyond our level of knowledge. This is the reason we must give our life and time to quality study of the Word and all materials that will enhance our self-improvement. When we are bejeweled by the precious stones of knowledge, we are approved by God and men for better opportunities and service.

## 3. Positive Confession

*"This book of the law shall not depart out of thy mouth; but thou shalt meditate therein day and night, that thou mayest observe to do according to all that is written therein: for then thou shalt make thy way prosperous, and then thou shalt have good success." Joshua 1:8*

Daily confession of the Word of God is one of the key habits God prescribed to Joshua. He told him to make sure the Book of the Law did not depart from his mouth; he was never to confess what God did not say in His Word. This requires a lot of discipline but it is the price we must pay to have the Word of God fulfilled in our lives. We need to realize that God gets things done by His spoken Word. What we say is what we see. God called light into existence at creation and light did appear. Through confession of God's Word, we can create our world. If we do not like what we see, we should confess what we would like to see. God saw darkness but wished for light and so He spoke light into existence. This is a fundamental principle of supernatural living. Like God, we must speak our destinies and purpose into existence.

## 4. Meditation

*"This book of the law shall not depart out of thy mouth; but thou shalt meditate therein day and night, that thou mayest observe to do according to all that is written therein: for then thou shalt make thy way prosperous, and then thou shalt have good success." (Joshua 1:8).*

To "meditate" means to pore over, to think over and over. The soul is the seat of our conscious existence. It houses our will, emotions and mind. Our level of prosperity is determined by what we do with this chamber of life. It is often said that he who captures the soul captures the entire being. When we yield our souls to the devil and his thoughts, evil ravages our personalities; but when our souls are given to meditating on the Word of God, God builds His stronghold in our souls and takes ownership of our souls.

We need to remember that our lives

gravitate in the direction of our thoughts. Godly thoughts will put God to work on our behalf and ensure the fulfillment of His purpose in our lives. It is needful to emphasize the significance of meditation as an important habit in the life of a believer by reproducing the words of the Psalmist on meditation:

*"Blessed is the man that walketh not in the counsel of the ungodly, nor standeth in the way of sinners, nor sitteth in the seat of the scornful. But his delight is in the law of the LORD; and in his law doth he meditate day and night. And he shall be like a tree planted by the rivers of water, that bringeth forth his fruit in his season; his leaf also shall not wither; and whatsoever he doeth shall prosper." (Psalms 1:1-3).*

## 5. Diligence

*"Seest thou a man diligent in his business? he shall stand before kings; he shall not stand before mean men." (Proverbs 22:29).*

To be diligent means to work at something energetically and devotedly, to be hardworking. God hates laziness but He rewards diligence. Hebrews 11:6 says He is a rewarder of those who diligently seek Him. For our purpose to be realized, we must tirelessly and enthusiastically work on it. Many purposes have been truncated by the virus called laziness. When God sees diligence, He rewards us with results.

## 6. Perseverance

*"Therefore, since we are surrounded by such a great cloud of witnesses, let us throw off everything that hinders and the sin that so easily entangles. And let us run with perseverance the race marked out for us."* *(Hebrews 12:1, NIV)*

The race of life is very intense and only those who will not quit win the race. It is sad that many people gave up when the finish line was within reach. Had they known how close they were to their breakthrough, they would have persevered just a little bit more. The question we need to ask ourselves whenever we are tempted to give up is "has God released me from this assignment?"

If he hasn't then whatever we do in the place of our purpose is done in futility; a total waste of time. I would rather keep on doing what He called me to do even though it seems not to be bearing much fruit than switch over to something different even if the different enterprise seems to be more rewarding and fruitful. I don't know which location you are at in the pursuit of your purpose, I will encourage you to shut your ears to all temptations to quit because quitters don't ever win.

## 7. Fasting & Prayer

*Moreover when ye fast, be not, as the hypocrites, of a sad countenance: for they disfigure their faces, that they may appear unto men to fast. Verily I say unto you, They have their reward. (Matthew 6:16)*

This verse presupposes that Jesus' disciples should live a fasted life. I do not mean we would fast every day. However, if we are led to fast every day, there is nothing wrong with doing so. What I mean is that the word 'When' (not "if") shows that Jesus expects his disciples to make fasting and prayer a habit. If Jesus fasted to fulfill His messianic ministry, I think he set for us a pattern of fasting as a means of fulfilling our purpose.

## 8. Sowing Into Other Peoples' Vision

*"The liberal soul shall be made fat: and he that watereth shall be watered also himself."* (Proverbs 11:25).

Great miracles do happen when we respond positively to the law of sowing and reaping. Whatever we want to see happen to us, we can make happen for other people. Joseph interpreted other people's dreams and his dream was fulfilled. Our purpose will never be fulfilled when we become so self-centered that we have no place for ministering to the needs of others. As we water other peoples' vision and dreams, ours will come to pass.

## 9. Worship And Putting God First

"But seek ye first the kingdom of God, and his righteousness; and all these things shall be added unto you." (Matthew 6:33).

We must never allow our God-given vision or purpose to take the place of God in our lives. No matter what, God remains God. We must put Him first in every area of our lives. Our fellowship with Him must take prime place above and beyond any other engagement in life. To put anything ahead of God is to make an idol of that thing. It might be good and commendable. It might be honorable and godly, but it is still not good enough to usurp the supreme place of God. Therefore our worship of Him and our personal devotional life must clearly stand at the top of our schedule. David was always in pursuit of God, and God helped him to fulfill his purpose beyond his wildest dream.

## 10. Humility

*"Likewise, ye younger, submit yourselves unto the elder. Yea, all of you be subject one to another, and be clothed with humility: for God resisteth the proud, and giveth grace to the humble. Humble yourselves therefore under the mighty hand of God, that he may exalt you in due time." (1 Peter 5:5-6).*

Humility is the garden in which the flowers of purpose blossom. The reason humility is so key to the fulfillment of purpose is that God demands it before He can help us accomplish His purpose for our lives. God Himself is incredibly humble. I wonder how a personality who owns the entire universe and more stoops so low to serve humanity. God is starkly humble; so humble to be born in a manger and so meek to be slaughtered on the Cross. Having set this example for us, he expects us to learn humility from Him. God will resist you if you are proud no matter how committed you are to His purpose for your life. Great people with promising future have made a shipwreck of their purpose in life because they were puffed up with pride. Pride led to the expulsion of Satan from Heaven, God has zero tolerance for pride. Many of us have been stuck in the mucky waters of pride which have impeded our race of destiny. We must always remember that in the Kingdom, the only way up is down. God resists the proud and gives grace (empowerment) to the humble.

## 11. Faithfulness

*"Moreover, it is required in stewards, that a man be found faithful. (1 Corinthians 4:2)*

To be faithful means to be reliable, trustworthy, dependable and loyal. Our purposes are so important to God that He will only accomplish them through people who are dependable and loyal to him. Many people who have been given great tasks in the kingdom have abandoned such tasks at the slightest opposition. When we have a vision from God Satan will unleash at us a flood of opposition and resistance designed to stifle the vision. In such situations, God expects us to be loyal both to Him and the purpose He has committed to us. We must be prepared to sacrifice all to please the one who has called us and when we are proved to be faithful, He will make sure our purpose is fulfilled.

## 12. Rest

*"When Jesus had spoken these words, he went forth with his disciples over the brook Cedron, where was a garden, into the which*

*he entered, and his disciples. And Judas also, which betrayed him, knew the place: for Jesus ofttimes resorted thither with his disciples".* (John 18:1-2)

The human body is designed to rest. It is true we are spirit beings but we need the human body to function on earth. If the human body dies, the purpose dies with it. We cannot afford to abuse our bodies and expect to live through the full course of time assigned to us by God. This is the reason we must practice rest on a daily basis. Jesus had a busy schedule but he made out time to rest. The verse quoted above shows that Jesus withdrew from time to time to take some rest at a garden by the side of brook Cedron. He rested whilst thousands were still seeking Him for ministry.

The truth is that needs will always be there, but our time on earth is limited. Consequently, we must keep our earthly clothing so that we can function optimally on earth while our time lasts. Balanced living is needful if we would fulfill our purpose;

we must have the wisdom to apportion our time between ministering to others and ministering to ourselves.

# CHAPTER 5

# FIGHT FOR YOUR PURPOSE

# *Fight For Your Purpose*

*"And you went over Jordan, and came unto Jericho: and the men of Jericho fought against you, the Amorites, and the Perizzites, and the* **Canaanites***, and the Hittites, and the Girgashites, the Hivites, and the Jebusites; and I delivered them into your hand."*
**—Joshua 24:11**

The fiercest battles on earth are the battles of destiny or purpose. Jesus was sacrificed on the altar of purpose. He died for the redemption of our souls. The nation of Israel was promised a land flowing with milk and honey but they had to fight through the stiffest oppositions to make that promise a reality.

Why do we have to fight for what is already ours? We must fight for all that God has given because we have an adversary who is prowling around seeking to disinherit us of the promise. Jesus says the thief comes to kill, steal and destroy (John 10:10). He will never be happy to see us taking possession of what God has promised us. God will always undertake for us because the battle is the Lord's but he wants us to take our place in faith and fight the good fight of faith. This is God's supreme wisdom. In the natural world, when a thief snatches our car and is about to drive it off, we don't kneel down in prayer and allow the thief drive the car off without a fight. We call the police; we seek help to recover what belongs to us.

In the same vein, if we believe the promise is ours, we will fight for it. It is not so much the engagement that matters as the faith which propels it.

In the above text, we see that God ultimately delivered the opposition into the hands of the children of Israel but He did not do so until they fought back in faith. Your purpose is one of the most treasured assets God has given to you and so it is the most haunted of all your endowments. It is your responsibility to guard it jealously. When it is taken, your life is left an empty shell; the substance is removed. Great men of God have shared their stories of great attacks and opposition when they set out to accomplish God's purpose for their lives. They became great because they fought back in faith and God in response to their faith gave them resounding victories.

Our passage above lists seven nations that stood in opposition to the children of Israel as they advanced to the Promised Land. Today, these seven nations are representative of the seven spiritual oppositions or obstacles we will encounter as we move to fulfill our purpose. These seven oppositions or obstacles are the handiwork of the spiritual forces enumerated in the Ephesians 6:12: "For we wrestle not against flesh and blood, but against principalities, against powers, against the rulers of the darkness of this world, against spiritual wickedness in high places."

These are the forces that stand stoutly against the fulfillment of our destiny and purpose. Even though these forces are five in number, they manifest in seven major ways in the nature of obstacles or oppositions to rob us of our purpose and destiny. With Israel, the battle was physical, with us it is spiritual. What are the seven obstacles the enemy through his demonic spirits puts on our path of destiny? They are as follow:

## The Spirit of Doubt

*"Now the serpent was more subtil than any beast of the field which the LORD God had made. And he said unto the woman, Yea,*

*hath God said, Ye shall not eat of every tree of the garden?" (Genesis 3:1).*

Adam and Eve were cheated out of their purpose when Eve succumbed to the spell of doubt cast upon her by the serpent. Satan will make us doubt everything we heard from God because he knows that without faith nothing gets done. This happens very often in the time of apparent delay in the fulfillment of the vision God has shown to us. He will introduce doubt into every department of our lives. He will make us doubt who we are in Christ. If we allow this cloud of doubt to persist, it is just a matter of time - what happened to Adam and Eve will happen to us.

## The Spirit of Limitation

*"Yea, they turned back and tempted God, and limited the Holy One of Israel. They remembered not his hand, nor the day when he delivered them from the enemy." (Psalms 78:41-42).*

The size of our vision or purpose could be intimidating. From the human standpoint, we cannot fulfill our purpose in our strength. Armed with this understanding, we need to trust and depend on God for the fulfillment of our purpose. The children of Israel were overwhelmed by the size of the vision and intimidated by the demands involved in the fulfillment of it. They were weighed down by a weight they were not designed to bear.

The vision or purpose is God's idea and God is more than able to bring it to pass. Our role is to trust Him for its fulfillment. Trouble arises when we get in His way and seek to fulfill the vision in our own strength and understanding. Israel limited God because in their limited understanding, there was no way they could make it to the Promised Land. They failed to allow God to be God. The result was fatal: the entire generation that limited God died in the wilderness.

The same fate befalls many visions today, when those given the vision by God get in God's way by trying to reason out the chances of its possibility. They fail to understand that with men, it will remain impossible but with God ALL THINGS ARE POSSIBLE.

## The Spirit of Slothfulness and Procrastination

*"By much slothfulness the building decayeth; and through idleness of the hands the house droppeth through." (Ecclesiastes 10:18).*

*"Yet a little sleep, a little slumber, a little folding of the hands to sleep: So shall thy poverty come as one that travelleth; and thy want as an armed man." (Proverbs 24:33-34).*

*"He that observeth the wind shall not sow; and he that regardeth the clouds shall not reap." (Ecclesiastes 11:4).*

Laziness and procrastination go hand in hand. What needs to be done must be done at the earliest opportunity. Excuses and waiting for the right time to get things done will only rob us of opportunities. What we need to do, we must do quick!

# The Spirit of Witchcraft and Divination

*"...And Balak the son of Zippor was king of the Moabites at that time. He sent messengers therefore unto Balaam the son of Beor to Pethor, which is by the river of the land of the children of his people, to call him, saying, Behold, there is a people come out from Egypt: behold, they cover the face of the earth, and they abide over against me: Come now therefore, I pray thee, curse me this people; for they are too mighty for me: peradventure I shall prevail, that we may smite them, and that I may drive them out of the land: for I wot that he whom thou blessest is blessed, and he whom thou cursest is cursed." (Numbers 22:4-6).*

*"And God said unto Balaam, Thou shalt not go with them; thou shalt not curse the people: for they are blessed." (Numbers 22:12).*

Satan can be confrontational when all his cunning devises fail. In the above verses, we see Satan moving a seer to cast a curse on Israel, contrary to God's will. With God's visible blessings hovering over Israel, the enemy still sought a way to put a curse on them. Unknown to the enemy, God's blessings are stronger than anyone's curses. The power of the blessing will supersede the curse at all times.

Sometimes, we need to actively resist the devil in spiritual warfare to prevent his curses from sticking to us. Witchcraft and divination are twin spirits by which many ministries are attacked. When they are in operation, we must stand in the place of authority against the devil and uproot his installations.

## The Spirit of "Grasshopper Mentality"

*"And they brought up an evil report of the land which they had searched unto the children of Israel, saying, The land, through which we have gone to search it, is a land that eateth up the inhabitants thereof; and all the people that we saw in it are men of a great stature. And there we saw the giants, the sons of Anak, which come of the giants: and we*

*were in our own sight as grasshoppers, and so
we were in their sight." (Numbers 13:32-34)*

Satan will either instigate you to inflate your
opinion of yourself with pride, or deflate
your confidence in Christ by inflicting you
with a spirit of inferiority complex. It is
true that in ourselves we can do nothing,
but we can do all things in Christ who
strengthens us. When God calls, He only
wants us to make ourselves available and
He will supply the ability. Our problem
stems from pitching our limited resources
against the huge challenges we face in the
way of fulfilling our purpose. Each time we
do this, we are dwarfed by the size of the
opposition. Let God face your Goliath and
the Goliath will fall face down.

## The Spirit of Fear

*"But the Egyptians pursued after them, all
the horses and chariots of Pharaoh, and his
horsemen, and his army, and overtook them
encamping by the sea, beside Pihahiroth,
before Baalzephon. And when Pharaoh drew
nigh, the children of Israel lifted up their*

*eyes, and, behold, the Egyptians marched after them; and they were sore afraid: and the children of Israel cried out unto the* LORD.*" (Exodus 14:9-10).*

*"For God hath not given us the spirit of fear; but of power, and of love, and of a sound mind." (2 Timothy 1:7).*

The spirit of fear freezes its victim into inaction. Israel was moving to the Promised Land when the forces of Egypt appeared behind them in a hot chase. The spirit of fear created so much pressure on them that they were distracted and apprehensive. Anybody who seeks to do something great for God must be ready to do battle against this spirit. We need the spirit of faith to do exploits for God, but Satan will afflict us with the spirit of fear to neutralize us. We must destroy the strongholds of fear to make progress for God. Remember, fear is more than a feeling; it is a spirit.

## The Spirit of Lust and Carnality

*"But with many of them God was not well pleased: for they were overthrown in*

*the wilderness. Now these things were our examples, to the intent we should not lust after evil things, as they also lusted. Neither be ye idolaters, as were some of them; as it is written, The people sat down to eat and drink, and rose up to play. Neither let us commit fornication, as some of them committed, and fell in one day three and twenty thousand. Neither let us tempt Christ, as some of them also tempted, and were destroyed of serpents. Neither murmur ye, as some of them also murmured, and were destroyed of the destroyer. Now all these things happened unto them for examples: and they are written for our admonition, upon whom the ends of the world are come." (1 Corinthians 10:5-11).*

Consecration is at the foundation of our walk with God. If we do not work on our carnal nature, it could rob us of our destiny. Spirituality is the highest level of prosperity; if we wallow in sin, every thought of fulfilling our purpose will be illusory. God is holy and all who seek to work for Him must be holy. God does not demand perfection;

all he requires from us is a hunger and thirst for righteousness. Thousands died in the wilderness because they took God for granted. Without holiness, our purpose may not see the light of the day. Satan will do all in his power to waylay us with his filthy garment but we must be determined to keep our garments white and unspotted at all times.

As we move toward the fulfillment of our purpose, we must be ready to uproot these obstacles by exercising our authority in Christ. When we walk in our God-given authority, God promises to bruise Satan under our feet and we will ultimately prevail.

*"And the God of peace shall bruise Satan under your feet shortly. The grace of our Lord Jesus Christ be with you. Amen." (Romans 16:20).*

# Prayer To Receive Jesus As Savior And Lord

ord Jesus, I acknowledge that I am a sinner. I believe and confess that you died on the cross for my sins and you were raised from the dead for my justification. Your Word says whosoever calls upon the name of the Lord shall be saved.

Today, I call upon your name; Lord Jesus, forgive me my sins and deliver me from the power of darkness. I receive you as my Savior and Lord. I renounce every control and dominion of Satan over my life.

Jesus, I thank you because according to your Word I am saved.

# NOTE

_____

_____

_____

_____

_____

_____

_____

_____

_____

_____

_____

_____

_____

# NOTE

_____

_____

_____

_____

_____

_____

_____

_____

_____

_____

_____

_____

_____

_____

## NOTE

_____

_____

_____

_____

_____

_____

_____

_____

_____

_____

_____

_____

_____

# NOTE

_____

_____

_____

_____

_____

_____

_____

_____

_____

_____

_____

_____

_____

_____

# NOTE

_____

_____

_____

_____

_____

_____

_____

_____

_____

_____

_____

_____

_____